Warsaw, IN:
A LONG TIME AGO

1938-1973

DALE LONG

WESTBOW
PRESS®
A DIVISION OF THOMAS NELSON
& ZONDERVAN

WestBow Press books may be ordered through booksellers or by contacting:

WestBow Press
A Division of Thomas Nelson & Zondervan
1663 Liberty Drive
Bloomington, IN 47403
www.westbowpress.com
844-714-3454

ISBN: 978-1-6642-6058-0 (sc)
ISBN: 978-1-6642-6057-3 (e)

Print information available on the last page.

WestBow Press rev. date: 04/11/2022

Introduction

How did this book ever come to be? I never saw myself as a writer and never ever thought about writing a book!

It began with a desire to preserve some of the stories of my growing-up years and what life was like back then, for my family and for future generations. At eighty-three years of age, as I've talked with younger people over time, I have realized that this period of history and the personal experiences of that time are almost lost. To many, they may not seem important, but my passion to share those memories continued to grow until I knew I *had* to write them down.

Will there be a sequel to this story? Maybe. I'm thinking about sharing some of the stories from my forty-five-year marriage to Karen and our family life. It will definitely be an adventure book!

This book is dedicated to my wonderful parents and family, and to anyone who has influenced my life in any way. You have been a part of my journey to become the man I am today, and for that, I am most grateful.

A very special thank you to Tierney Boggs, who has invested hours and hours helping us through this process to bring my story to life.

What's *your* story?

Baby Dale

Dale, age two

School Days

ooo

Warsaw, Indiana, was a small town of about six thousand people. The city limits were about seven blocks from the courthouse in three directions. It was longer on the east side and connected with another small town called Winona Lake.

We had five schools within the city limits, including East Ward, West Ward, and Center Ward. That makes them sound more like prisons than schools. There was also a freshman high and a senior high. If you lived outside the city limits, you rode the bus to West Wayne or East Wayne schools for grades one through five. You went to Center Ward for sixth grade.

West Ward School was built on N. Union Street in 1872. This site is now occupied by the Madison Elementary School.

West Ward

I walked to West Ward for first through fifth grade. It was a two-story brick building. First, second, and fifth grades were on the first floor. Third and fourth grades were on the second floor. There was also a small area for the custodian, who kept the fire going in the furnace.

There was one bathroom with one stool and one sink. We were to use the bathroom only for emergencies. We were to go to the bathroom before we walked into the school building at eight o'clock. Lunch was from eleven to noon. We walked home and back. School was out at three in the afternoon. I would leave school each day and do my paper route, which I had from age six to age fourteen.

Sometimes, in fifth grade, I would run my route and return to school to pitch softball. I had a really nice raise/curve ball that would cause a pop-up. Earl Snell had bad eyes and played right field. We would have to tell him which way to go to get the ball. He was a neat guy.

We played a lot of running and tag. I was the fastest runner in my class. Dennis Mulcachy and Sally Parren were always on my tail. I have loved to run ever since then.

In the third and fourth grades, I would bring small snakes to school and let them out in class. Martha Fawley was fun to scare.

Close to my home was a factory named Kimble Glass. It produced small, cigar-shaped glass tubes. I would get some hydrogen sulfide, fill a tube, and take it to school. Then, before recess, I would open it up and put it in the wastebasket. When we came back in, the room would smell like rotten eggs.

When I was in about the fourth grade, my brother, Max (who was in the eighth or ninth grade), started playing trombone in band. He took lessons for it. Mom and Dad decided to get me a baritone, which was almost the same size as I was. I took lessons like Max did and learned to make the right sounds come out of it.

I knew how to read music by what line the note was on and which fingers to hold down to make the three different levels of sound. If the note was solid black, I held the note for one beat; if the note was open in the middle, I held it for two beats; and if it had a little flag on it, I just played it really quick.

I would sometimes carry the big thing to West Ward and play it. I never actually learned what each note was called. When I was in the sixth grade, the band instructor would stop the band on more than one occasion and say, "Dale, would you play me a G?"

I would ask, "What finger do I use for that?"

Sometimes he would just reply, "Dale, sit this song out and just pretend you are playing your horn."

Dale, *front row center*; **Sonya,** *front row, far-right*

In the third grade, there was a very cute girl named Sonya Echert. She kissed me in the classroom when we were alone. Nice! In our third-grade class picture, she was the one with flowers in her hand looking my way with a gleam in her eye. She moved to Sydney, Indiana, and later in life became a nurse.

Mr. Jones

The five years at West Ward were great. It was during WWII, and most of the men were off fighting. We had all women teachers for first through fifth grades. The fifth-grade teacher was the principal and had a paddle that she didn't hesitate to use.

We had a twenty-minute recess midmorning and another one midafternoon. When recess was over, the first-grade teacher would ring her little bell, which meant to pick up everything and get in a straight line, not talking or touching anyone. We would march into our classroom and sit quietly with our hands folded on top of our desks. We did that every day.

The year we went into fifth grade, the woman principal retired, and Foster Jones, who was also our fifth-grade teacher, became the new principal. He was an older guy and also a farmer. A man with a paddle was frightening to us guys. We were all trying to adjust to the changes.

One day, we were out at recess playing softball. Mr. Jones came out and was umpiring for us. We'd never had an umpire before. We were doing well until the first-grade teacher rang the bell. We all headed for our lines, but Mr. Jones said, "Wait a minute. We have two more outs to go before we go in."

Dale, fifth grade

Wonderful! The four other teachers realized this guy was going to be a problem.

Each month, Mr. Jones would take the best row in his class to his farm for a hot dog roast. He kept moving me around until I was in a row with all girls. That worked. It seems I behaved better around the girls than I did around the guys!

Carolyn Philips was a girl in my fifth-grade class. In the class picture, she has on a Girl Scout uniform with a hat. She was always nice to me, so I thought I'd marry her someday.

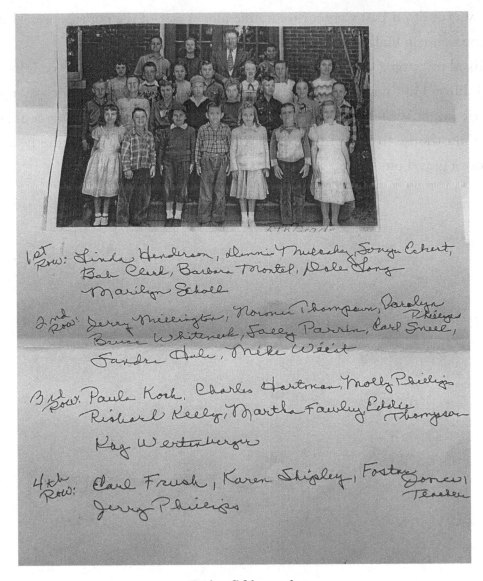

1st Row: Linda Henderson, Dennis Mulcahy, Sonya Cohort, Bob Clark, Barbara Montel, Dale Long, Marilyn Scholl

2nd Row: Jerry Millington, Norman Thompson, Carolyn Phillips, Bruce Whitenack, Sally Parvin, Carl Snell, Sandra Hale, Mike Weist

3rd Row: Paula Koch, Charles Hartman, Molly Phillips, Richard Kelly, Martha Fawley, Eddie Thompson, Kay Wertenberger

4th Row: Earl Frush, Karen Shipley, Foster Jones, Teacher, Jerry Phillips

Dale, fifth grade

Scouting

Mother took me to the Evangelical United Brethren (EUB) church on West Center Street, one block west of the courthouse. A new church, Trinity United Brethren

Church, was built on East Center Street nine blocks east of the courthouse. This EUB church took part in Cub Scouts and Boy Scouts.

We liked to camp a lot. The best place to camp was on Fox Farm Road, by a place called McElroy Hill. Back then, it was quite the hill. The east side went way up six to eight stories high. We felt like we were camping on top of the world. You could see the Warsaw Courthouse from there. Later, this side was dug out to make the new US 30 and is now a gravel pit.

Growing Up at 774 West Center Street

Mom in our garden

Max, Dale, and Dad with tractor

My Brother, Max

I had an older brother named Max who was five years older than me. Before starting school, I worked in the garden with Mother. Max and I would take a wagonful of vegetables and go up and down the street selling them. We would collect old papers and junk and take them to the scrapyard and sell them for a penny a pound. We would then go to the mom-and-pop Jet White Grocery for a treat or save our money to go to the movies at the Strand Theater. A movie cost twelve cents and popcorn cost five cents.

Max and I were out cutting weeds one day, and he had this large tool called a sickle

Max and Dale

cutter. He told me to stand back, but I didn't do it fast enough. It cut my right leg really badly. I still have the scar to prove it.

Max was smarter than me, but I had talents in other areas. He took me bowling one time, and I beat his score. Both of us ended up working at the bowling alley. We were pinsetters. When the ball hit the pins, we would jump down, pick up the pins, reset them, and send the bowling ball back to the players. Not a fun job. Kind of a headache (literally) at times!

Max and Eddie Johnson (a neighbor boy who was Max's age) would go rabbit hunting with .410 shotguns. Both guns were bolt-action. They could shoot two to three times faster than I could with my single shotgun. I would wait until they made their shots and the rabbit had stopped and made a turn to go through a fence for cover. I got more rabbits than they did!

As we grew up, Dad didn't want Max or me to work where he did, so we each went our own ways. After his time as a paperboy like me, Max ran a linotype machine at the *Times Union* newspaper in Warsaw. He served in the USAF in Texas before moving to Anderson, Indiana, and working for Delco Remy.

When Dad died, Max came and took all of Dad's shop equipment. When Max retired and moved to Denver, Colorado, he packed all of Dad's tools in an old school bus and moved them with him. He never unloaded a lot of the stuff. If there was something he wanted, he would just break a window and get it. He donated most of Dad's shop equipment to a school out there.

Dale, Merlin, Max and Lura Long

My Grandparents, Phoebe and Charley "Pickle" Long

My grandmother Phoebe and grandfather Charley "Pickle" Long lived next door. When I would come home from school, Phoebe would often yell out the window, "Daley, come over for some sugar cookies." Best cookies in the world! The problem was that she would give me milk to drink with the cookies. She had cans of Milnot milk that she mixed with water. It was terrible stuff!

Grandpa was an old logger and mowed yards and cut down trees for a living. I would help him do both. He had one of those two-man saws. I ran one end and he ran the other. Sometimes I had to run my end lying under a house. He could fell a tree right where he wanted it.

Grandpa bought me my first .22 rifle. It shot two kinds of bullets:.22 shorts and .22 longs. The shorts had just a little powder in them.

This rifle had a firing pin that you pulled down to put the shell in and then flipped it up against the back of the shell. You were then ready to pull the hammer back and pull the trigger to fire. You had to pull the firing pin down again to take the old shell out. With the .22 long rifle shell, you pulled the trigger and quickly moved your head away from the gun because the old shell came flying out the back and would hit you in the eye.

Grandma and Grandpa Long

I had a lot of BB guns to shoot snakes and frogs and cans and bottles and birds. I got in trouble one time for shooting birds. We mostly liked to shoot sparrows. One day I accidentally hit a jenny wren, and a neighbor called the police. The policeman showed up at my house, took my best BB gun, and told me to come up and see him in a week or two.

It was a long two weeks, but finally it was time to go to the fire station where his office was upstairs. He said it was lunchtime, so I walked beside him and his big gun to the Breading Cigar Store. I sat beside him and the gun. He bought my lunch, and we went back to his office.

I got a lecture and my gun back. When I was fourteen, I worked at the Breading Cigar Store, serving food and selling cigars.

We lived next to a swamp with lots of frogs, snakes, and rats. Five houses from the city dump down on West Center Street, there was something called the *inner urban rail car*. It ran by our house past the dump and across the river where the city sewers ran out into the river.

Grandpa was down there one day setting some traps for animals. Max and I were with him. He got caught in quicksand and couldn't get out. Max got a pole for him to hang on to, and I ran a half mile for help. That was scary!

Growing Up with Mom

Lura Long was my amazing mother. When I was thirteen, my dad received a large bottle of Mogen David wine for Christmas from Zimmer's, where he worked. There was no drinking allowed in my home, but Mom felt she couldn't just throw it out, so she put it on a high shelf on the back porch.

Over a period of a few months, Mom said it looked like the wine was slowly evaporating. She knew Dad wouldn't drink it, and my brother had moved out, so it was either Mom or me. I think you can guess who the culprit was!

Whenever I left the house, no matter how old I was, Mom *always* said, "Be good, Dale. Just be good!" Hmm … what did she know about me that I didn't know she knew?

Lura Long and Grandma Bowman

Mom's maiden name was Lura Bowman. Her parents, Dan and Cora Bowman, owned a diner that had been a railroad car at one time, as well as a gas station west of Warsaw along Old US 30, about where the Creighton Brothers plant is now. The diner was about two hundred feet off the Pennsylvania Railroad.

When they moved to Warsaw, my mother and grandmother did the cooking for Warsaw High School, which was just one block from West Ward School on West Main Street. I also had lunch at the high school and hand-wrapped the silverware.

When I was about to be born at Murphy Medical Center in Warsaw on December 8, 1938, my mother told Dad to go back to work. She was a very practical woman, and all a husband could do during the delivery was pace back and forth in the hallway. Besides, she had done this before five years earlier with my brother, Max. Dad complied and left to go back to work at Zimmer's.

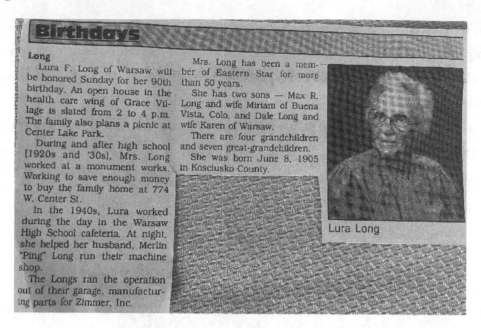

Birthdays

Long

Lura F. Long of Warsaw will be honored Sunday for her 90th birthday. An open house in the health care wing of Grace Village is slated from 2 to 4 p.m. The family also plans a picnic at Center Lake Park.

During and after high school (1920s and '30s), Mrs. Long worked at a monument works. Working to save enough money to buy the family home at 774 W. Center St.

In the 1940s, Lura worked during the day in the Warsaw High School cafeteria. At night, she helped her husband, Merlin "Ping" Long run their machine shop.

The Longs ran the operation out of their garage, manufacturing parts for Zimmer, Inc.

Mrs. Long has been a member of Eastern Star for more than 50 years.

She has two sons — Max R. Long and wife Miriam of Buena Vista, Colo. and Dale Long and wife Karen of Warsaw.

There are four grandchildren and seven great-grandchildren.

She was born June 8, 1905 in Kosciusko County.

Lura Long

Today, young people may not remember famous cowboys like Roy Rogers and Dale Evans and the Lone Ranger. My mother didn't know if I would be a boy or a girl. She gave me the first name Dale, middle name Roy, and last name Long, which was close to *Lone Ranger.* That also made my initials D. R. Long, or Dr. Long for short. My brother's name was Max Robert Long, which made him Mr. Long. OK, enough of that!

My bedroom was about eight feet by eight feet, up some very curvy stairs. For my birthday each year, Mom baked my favorite cake—angel food. I ate most of it myself, a little at a time, so sometimes it was getting a little stale by the time I finished it. I often walked in my sleep and would even walk down those steep curvy stairs during the night to get something to eat.

One year after my birthday, I walked down to the kitchen to get a piece of that angel food cake Mom had baked for me. I was still half asleep. This time, I didn't it eat it all on the way back to bed. The next morning, after a not-so-good night's sleep, I discovered I had been rolling all night on cake crumbs! I don't ever remember sleepwalking again.

We had a coal-burning stove in the living room. As far as a phone, we had a party line that we shared with neighbors. There was no TV. The only other means of communication was the AM radio, which usually had a lot of static.

Our kitchen had a gas stove but no microwave. Instead of what we now call a refrigerator, we had an icebox, which had a compartment in the top part where we placed a chunk of ice to keep the food cold. A truck would come by once a week, and we would put a sign in the front window saying what size chunk of ice we needed. The food sat next to the chunk of ice as it melted slowly over the next few days.

We had a large garden that I helped with, and Mom did a lot of canning. We put other food in the cellar to keep cool. People back then were pretty self-sufficient.

On December 7, 1941, the day before my third birthday, Pearl Harbor was bombed, which propelled the United States into World War II. When the war broke out, all kinds of problems came up. We had this thing called blackouts. The United States was afraid of being bombed by planes coming over the North Pole and across Canada. We could be hit within one hour from the US/Canada border. There was no radar or anything else to warn us. We just listened to the radio.

We were digging bomb shelters during the day, and when the sun went down, everyone was to be home and in the house with their blinds closed. All roads and streets were closed. All gas stations, food stores, and restaurants were closed. All streetlights and stoplights were turned off, as well as the courthouse's and the Lake City Bank's clock lights. There were no trucks or trains running. The idea was that if we were ever a target, the enemy would not be able to see the town.

Police had people walking around at night, and if they saw light in your window, they would pound on your door. We would sit and play cards by candlelight and listen to the radio. Note: we all had rights back then, too, but nobody complained or went out at night.

Growing up, the neighborhood kids and I spent a lot of time playing at the city dump, which was only seven houses west of our home on Center Street. We really liked to shoot glass bottles with our BB guns there. One day, while we were playing, I found a shoebox. When I opened it, I found a brand new pair of women's shoes. I took them home to my mom, and she said they were nice shoes, but the left one was a different size than the right one.

Yet when she tried them on, she exclaimed that they fit perfectly! She'd always had a hard time finding shoes because one of her feet was larger than the other one. She wore those shoes for many years.

My grandmother Cora's father was a doctor. Dr. Gaskell had a cure for skin cancer made with a mixture of flowers and weeds that his wife, who was Indian, had taught him how to make. Cora and my mother would go with him to apply the mixture. His business card said Doctor Gaskell—Cancer Cure—Bourbon, IN.

Mom said he was a quack doctor, because he had no license to be a doctor. But the mixture still worked. Unfortunately, the formula was never passed down to me!

After the war, we got a seventeen-inch black-and-white TV with three stations, which were only on part of the time. If the TV did not work right, you had to take eight or ten tubes out of

Lura Long

the back and take them to the drugstore to test on their tester, and then buy whatever new replacement tubes you needed.

At eight or nine years old, I started a savings account at the bank with my income of five dollars a week from my paper route. Mom would let me walk uptown to go to the movies at the Strand or Centennial movie theaters. It would be dark when it was over.

There were only two phones in town. There was one phone at the courthouse corner and another at the Breading Cigar Store. When the movie was over, I would call Mom and tell her I was starting to run home. She said she would walk up the street to meet me.

I would run the seven blocks home as fast as I could, reciting the twenty-third Psalm as I ran. I would meet Mom one house from where we lived. I was fast!

One night, when the leaves were off the trees and there was a full moon out, it looked like the moon was moving as fast as I was. Once I reached Mom, the moon seemed to stand still once again. Whew!

Mom and Dad

Mom was a Bible-reading churchgoer, and we went every Sunday to Trinity United Brethren Church on East Center Street. She held a record at church for the most times reading completely through the Bible. She received a special certificate for that.

She drove to church in our one car. Dad never went to church. He worked in his machine shop behind our house instead.

Mom and I would drive to church and walk in together. She would go to the church service, and I would go to my Sunday school class. Sometimes, I managed to get by the Sunday school teacher and head out the other door. I would go across the street to the gas station to play the pinball machine for five cents a game, and then I'd wait for Mom in the car. However, there were a lot of times I didn't make it past the teacher!

There were only two pinball machines in town. As some of the boys and I got older, we would ride our bikes to Atwood, a town seven miles west, in less than an hour, and we'd play pinball at the gas station. I was a great bike rider—no hands, my feet on the handlebars, sitting backward and jumping ramps.

Mom played the piano and would sometimes play at the movie theater during silent films. She had a part-time job during the day and also worked on a job Dad set up for her in his workshop behind the garage. Dad was a machinist/tool and die maker, and he had an engine lathe, drill press, tool grinder, and turret lathe. Mom ran the turret lathe.

Mom and Dad

She put a twelve-inch wire (about a quarter as thick as a pencil) in the lathe. Then she pulled the lever down and put a groove in the wire. She moved to the next spot and pulled the lever again. Each time, she made a small groove in the wire, one inch apart. The wires were stainless steel and very strong. It was a measuring instrument used by doctors.

She was paid good money for doing it. Dad worked in the shop every night also making things for doctors. That's how Zimmer's got started.

Mom in shop

Dad

His name was Merlin J. Long. At work, they called him Ping. His dad, Charley Long, was called Pickle. Mom and Dad had a good marriage—just different. I never saw them kiss or say "I love you" or hug or say "Have a nice day." They never held hands or sat at the table and prayed. I'm not sure how my brother and I were ever conceived!

Dad, Company L Army

Before I was born, Dad worked for the Kosciusko County Highway Department. He helped make most of the county dirt roads. He was also a member of the Company L Army. It was kind of like the National Guard is now. He had a US uniform and would spend two weeks each summer at Camp Atterbury in southern Indiana.

Merlin J. Long

Zimmer's started out making flexible splints for broken arms. As a tool and die maker, Dad worked in his shop out back making prototype tools for doctors to try. They would try them and if they liked them, Zimmer's would then manufacture them.

He invented quite a few other things for Zimmer's but didn't patent them, so he never received any recognition or money for them.

When Dad started working at Zimmer's, this became our daily schedule: When Dad got up, Mom had breakfast ready for him and his lunch packed. By six in the morning, Dad was off to work at Zimmer's. As Zimmer's first foreman, he was the first one there to open up and get work set up for the day for all the other shop workers.

He closed the shop up about five in the evening. When he got home, Mom had supper ready for him, and then he went out to his workshop behind the garage. If it was cold outside, he would build a fire in the shop stove.

He worked until nine o'clock. Then he came up to the house to wash up and drive to town to Breading's Cigar Store, where he would smoke and play dominoes until ten at night.

Dad in his machine shop

Dad playing cards with Zimmer friends

Since Dad worked so much in the evenings, Mom and I spent about every evening together. We never ate with Dad at the table. Max was five years older and had his own friends and activities, so it was just mom and me. She read to me and we watched something on one of the three stations we had on TV, like *What's My Line*, *Fibber McGee and Molly*, or *The Shadow Knows*.

The only time Dad and Max were with Mom and me in the evenings was during the blackouts in 1941–1942. On Saturdays, Dad worked in the shop all day. On Sunday, he worked in the shop until noon. He never went to church with us. He had a large birthmark on the right side of his forehead, and one time someone at church had made a bad remark about it, and he would never go back

Sunday afternoon was family time. We all got in the car and drove out of town a little way and then circled back home after about fifteen or twenty miles. We did take one trip to the Smoky Mountains.

Dad pole-vaulting

There are several pictures of Dad when he was growing up that showed he was in sports. Yet neither he nor Mom ever came to any of my sporting events. He did buy me a new bike every two years for my paper route and a pair of track shoes once.

Dale with new bike, age fourteen   **Dale with new bike, age nine**

My dad liked to fish more than anything else when he had time. Once a year, we would take a vacation and rent a cabin on a lake within about fifty miles. The four of us—Mom, Dad, Max, and I—would get in the boat right after breakfast and fish until noon. We would come in for lunch and go back out to fish all afternoon. Mom would fish and read.

In the evening, Dad would clean the fish. We ate fish every night. Dad worked so much that we didn't enjoy a lot of family time together, so these memories are very special.

Dale and Dad fishing

Fishing trip

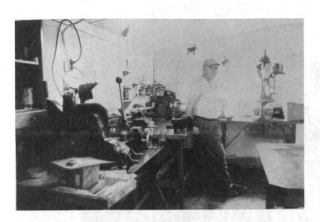

Dad in old machine shop   **Dad at Zimmer's machine shop**

When I was sixteen, Mom, Dad, and Grandma and Grandpa Bowman built a home on the southwest side of Winona Lake. Dad put his machine shop in the garage. It was a nice home, and Dad could fish right outside standing in the front yard.

Dan Bowman, Cora Bowman and Lura Long

Merlin Long

Early Jobs

Paper Route

I had three different *Times Union* paper routes, plus at times, Ronald Sharp would pick me up and take me to sell papers at halftime at school basketball tournaments. Papers were five cents, and I got half of the profit plus a new paper bag.

Dale

TIMES CARRIERS ENJOY CHICAGO TRIP.—Left to right: Back row: Jean Wuthrich, Milford, Larry King, Pierceton, Pat Finton Syracuse, Earl Ruihley, Warsaw, Philip Worth, Syracuse, Sandy Diehl, Leesburg, Virgil Wuthrich, Milford, Tommy Kenner, Pierceton, Beverly Klingerman and Shirley Savage, Cromwell.
Second row left to right: Jimmy White, North Webster, Thames Hickman, Wilmot, Cary Sloan, Warsaw, Denny Keener, Pierceton Kieth Grindle, Syracuse, Billy Deafenbaugh, Sally Wyman, J. Hawk, Dale Long, Warsaw.
Front row: George Bowler, Milford Junction, Alan Wuthrich, Milford, Robert Huffer, Eddie Murray, Don Truex, George Knee, Gary Niemann, Carleton Woodworth, Warsaw.
Joe Shoemaker, Mentone, Delorts and Dorothy Hogan, Etna Green, and Marvin and Melvin Fuller, of Tippecanoe, were picked up on the way to the game and do not appear in the picture. (Mowrey Photo Service).

Trip to the ball game with the Times Union

Trip to the ballgame with the *Times Union*

I received the title of Carrier of the Year one time for the *Times Union*. They would take the top carriers to Chicago in a bus once a year to a Cubs or White Sox ballgame. I went at least five times.

This was before interstates, so we drove right through South Chicago. Can you imagine a busload of boys from Warsaw with the windows down yelling at Black people? It was indeed a different time in history, and we really didn't know any better.

On my second route, at nine years old, I had a short route of about twelve blocks. On block two, I had the Murphy Medical Center Hospital, which received at least twelve to fifteen papers per day. That was literally a load off my shoulders.

The third route was the best—downtown Warsaw at ages ten to fourteen. I would deliver the paper inside the Lake Theater and sometimes sit down to rest and watch whatever movie was playing. I must have seen *The Greatest Show on Earth* about ten times.

Dale   Max Truex, Olympian runner

Max Truex, Olympian runner

GAME FOR THE WINNERS—Here are the Times- Union carrier contest winners who recently attended an American league baseball game at Comiskey park, Chicago, between the Chicago White Sox and the Boston Red Sox.

Pictured left to right the carriers are:

Back row—Virgil Wuthrich, Milford, Bob Likens, North Webster, Tommy Keener and Larry King, Pierceton, and Richard Van Cleave and Jerry Schaaf, Warsaw.

Second row—Jimmy White, North Webster, Allen Wuthrich, Milford, Mona Bauer, Warsaw, Gertrude Buntain, Larwill, and Billy Deafenbaugh Tommy Hoover, Cary Sloan, Carlton Woodworth and Max Truex, Warsaw.

Front row—Phillip Neff, Claypool, Marvin Sponhauer, Collomer, Sally Wyman, Warsaw Denny Hammond, Liberty Mills, and Dale Long and Jay Hawk, Warsaw.—(Photo by Mowrey Studio, Warsaw.

Dale

Also on South Buffalo Street, there were two beer joints side by side. I sold a lot of papers there and got nice tips from all the drunks.

Above the beer joint, at the corner of Market Street and South Buffalo, just above the large word *Warsaw*, was a bunch of apartments used by locals. The lady who ran the place was Mrs. Black. I never saw a Mr. Black. She had all her black curtains pulled shut, and she always wore black clothes.

Times-Union Junior Merchant

May 1950

DALE LONG, 11, son of Mr. and Mrs. Merlin Long, of 774 West Center street, is one of the youngest and smallest Times-Union carriers in Warsaw. He is four feet, eight inches tall, weighs 77 pounds, and has dark brown hair and blue eyes.

"Longie," as he is known among the other carriers, has been a "little merchant" for five years, starting at the age of six as a sub for his brother, Max, now employed in the Times-Union mailing department. For the past two years he has had his own route, and believes his experience as a carrier has taught him "how to deal with the public and to be a business-like boy." His route work is supervised by his parents, and from the proceeds of the "little business" the lad has established a savings account.

Dale has many other interests—he plays the baritone in the junior high school band; participates in basketball, baseball and track; likes to skate; does wood carving, and is a member of the Evangelical United Brethren church and the Boys club. Following his graduation from high school, he plans to realize his ambition—he wants to be a newspaperman.

I delivered her paper daily. The paper was twenty-five cents per week for six days of paper delivery, and collection was on Friday. Mrs. Black would pat me on the head and give me a ten cent tip each week if I would sit down with her and listen as she read the Bible to me.

Really! She did this for two years. She even told me the day Jesus was coming back. When that day came and passed, she said she was sorry, and she would look into it more.

A half block south was Dr. Baker's dentist office. On collection day, he would ask me if I wanted the twenty-five cents or to have a tooth filled. I ate a lot of chocolate, so Mom said get them filled.

This small building was located at 214 S. Buffalo Street for over 100 years. It was a doctor's office in the early 1900s, and then J.I. Baker operated his dental office there for almost 50 years. The building was demolished in 1996.

Just across the alley was Wolford's Electric Appliance Store. Mr. and Mrs. Wolford owned the store. He was an electrician.

My wonderful mother liked to make me toast. She had the kind of toaster that was shaped somewhat like a pyramid. She would set the toaster on the stove with four pieces of bread propped up on the sides of the toaster. She had to turn the bread over at just the right time or it would burn.

I wanted to buy Mom a new toaster for Christmas. Mrs. Wolford said if I would buy a loaf of bread and leave it there, we would try a different toaster each time I came in. It took two loaves of bread to get the job done. I must have made the right choice, as we had that toaster for years. Can you imagine doing that now?

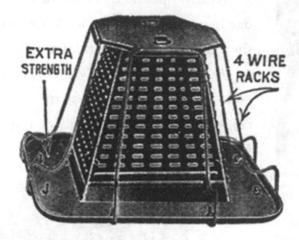

Vintage toaster

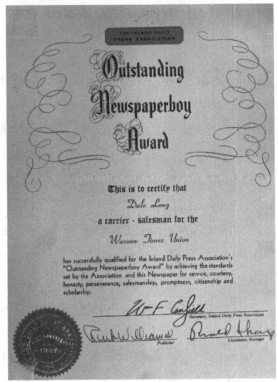

Favorite Café Restaurant

75 Years Ago

75 Years Ago

Fritz Wolferman made a gallant return to the pitching box as Warsaw's A. A. team turned back the Goshen All-Stars by score of 8 to 5.

The game, played at the local softball field before a small crowd that braved a cold wind and light rain, was Warsaw's second Northern Indiana league battle. The locals had previously lost their league opener at Plymouth.

Goshen's defending state champions took a 1 to 0 lead in the second inning, but the locals came right back in their half of the inning and tied the score.

I worked at the Favorite Café when I was twelve and thirteen. Tip Walker was the owner at the time. I was the dishwasher, busboy, table-cleaner, waiter for the people at the counter, and cashier. I also went next door in the alley to the Unique Bakery to get the fresh pies and rolls for the day. They had a big barrel of walnuts, and I would grab a handful as I left.

I enjoyed making chocolate malts and eating the leftover pie at the end of the day, not wanting any food to go to waste. It certainly didn't go to waste on me! I put on thirty pounds in two years. I went from 90 to 120 pounds!

I also enjoyed working with the waitresses, but once in a while there was a problem with them. Regulars would leave a tip for the girls, but occasionally a customer would forget. Then when I cleaned the table, it would look like I stole their tip.

One of my older classmates, Earl Frush, was one of the cooks. When our school basketball team had an

75 Years Ago

Warsaw's A. A. softball team, holders of third place in the northern Indiana League, staged a big uprising in the seventh inning at Wabash to beat the Wabash Moose, 8-6.

Trailing 6-5 as they came to bat in the seventh, the locals exploded with a devastating hitting attack. Gabby Garber started things off with a double and scored the tying run on Ab Shively's double. Then Merl Shively singled his brother home and, after Fred Gilliam popped out, Lew Goshert drove in another run with a single.

Warsaw was credited with 11 hits and one error.

out-of-town game, Earl and I fixed them food and had them come in to eat. It was usually a cheeseburger and fries in a small basket and a paper cup for their drink. No dishes to wash!

Earl had a Cushman motor scooter. One time we rode it out of town to see a movie starring Marilyn Monroe and Jane Russell—*Gentlemen Prefer Blondes*. I never dated a blonde, so I really didn't know if that movie was true or not.

Softball

At about that same age, I volunteered to work with Gabby Garber from the WRSW radio station to run the electric scoreboard for the adult men's softball team called the Double A's. I got to sit up in the score box with Gabby while I operated the scoreboard, which was out in center field for all to see. The games were played in the evenings across the street from the Center Lake Pavilion on Canal Street. Some of the players were my dad, Ping Long; Shorty Piper; Abe Shively; Merl Shively; Gabby Garber; Fritz Wolferman; Fred Gilliam; and Lew Goshert.

It was fast-pitch softball, and the pitcher I liked most would stand on top of the mound and wave his arm in backward circles three times. Then, as he stepped forward to pitch, he went into a forward pitching motion, swinging his arm forward three times, letting go of the ball on the first or second or maybe even third rotation. The batter had to pay close attention to when the ball was actually released.

We had just one umpire, Bill Bahan, also known as Claw Hammer. He called all the balls and strikes as well as any plays made on any base. There were many arguments about his calls—from both sides! He retired at the end of the year, and after that you would see him walking around town with dark glasses and a cane. Maybe that explained some of his calls.

High School Years

Dale

Warsaw High School 1954

Dale

I had some trouble in ninth grade. I was a track star and very fast. I liked to run the mile with a runner named Max Truex, who was two years older, and who later qualified to run in the 1964 Tokyo Olympics.

He had the Warsaw record for the mile run at 4:27. We would run together a lot. He was five-foot-five, and when he ran with the big guys, he would take three steps to their one step. He looked like that bird in cartoons called the Road Runner. I always ran beside him or right behind him. I was about five-foot-seven, but I could never beat him.

In one race with him, I got the inside lane, and he got the outside lane. I thought that maybe if I could get out in front of him, he would run behind me for a change. The gun went off, and off I went as hard as I could go. This was a mile run, and as I made the first curve, I could almost feel him right behind me.

I continued down the back stretch of the quarter-mile track. Finally, I decided to cut back to see if he would stay in back of me—only to find it was not Max but some other guy. Max had passed me at the quarter-mile mark and said, "What in the world is wrong with you today?"

So much for trying to beat Max Truex! Dad would buy me new track shoes, but Mom and Dad and my brother never came to see me run.

Track medal

My regular English teacher was on maternity leave, so we got a new teacher who was an English major just out of college. One day, I came into class a little late. I'd had some trouble and had to go see the principal for a bit. The principal and the school nurse were in the same area.

As I came into class, the teacher jumped on me about being late. I told her I had been in the principal's office. She asked if anyone knew where the girl who sat in front of me was. I said the girl was in the nurse's office sick, with dry heaves and a red face.

The teacher said, "No, she's not *sick*."

We went back and forth a few times. What she was trying to tell me was that the proper word to use was *ill*, not *sick*. She thought I was being disrespectful, but I really didn't know the difference. I had always used the word *sick*.

She gave me an F, which took me off the track team, the one thing about school that I loved and was really good at doing. Without track, I became a rebel without a cause for the rest of high school. Strange I still remember her name.

Also in my freshman year, we were all sent home on June 2, 1953, to watch Queen Elizabeth II be crowned Queen of England. I had plans to do something else with that free time, but Mom insisted otherwise. We watched it together on our nineteen-inch black-and-white TV, and I'm glad we did. It was great then, and it means even more now looking back.

The year before (1952), we got out of school for two hours to go to the train station on the east/west track as Eisenhower's train stopped. He was running for president and spoke from the last car on the train. Those stops were called "whistle stops." His wife didn't like to fly, so if she came along, it had to be by train.

MACHINE SHOP IN OPERATION. — Senior high school boys take the advanced machine shop course. It prepares them to take their place in some type of industrial, automotive or repair work.

Age Fourteen

Life was getting better. My paper route paid me five dollars a week, and Favorite Café fifty cents per hour. Next, I worked at the Breading Cigar Store for seventy-five cents an hour.

There were two Breading Cigar Stores. The first one had what were called *spittoons*. If you were chewing tobacco, you just spit in one of them on the floor. It also had a sign in the front window advertising a soft drink called Spur. It was like Sprite, but better!

Chapter 9 — 1920 to 1929

Employees stand in front of the W.B. Yost Cigar Store at 114 E. Center Street in the early 1900s. Employee Robert Breading purchased the business and changed the name to Breading's Cigar Store.

A 25¢ token for Breading's Cigar Store.

Breading's Cigar Store

In the 1920s, Robert Breading, Sr. and his son, Lewis "Peanuts," started Breading's Cigar Store in a two-story wood frame building at 114 E. Center Street on the east side of the alley. The business then moved into its current location in 1950 at 116 E. Center Street.

The Breading's store was a popular gathering place for breakfast and lunch. Dominoes was such a favorite pastime there that tournaments were held. Some even played hearts, euchre, and other games with dominoes.

Opening at 5:00 a.m. and not closing sometimes until 2:00 a.m. the next morning, Breading's quickly became known as the place to call or stop by for the latest news and sporting event updates. When the Moose, Eagles, Elks, and other lodges closed after midnight, Breading's was where everyone went for an early morning breakfast.

The Breading men sold the business to Ray Deafenbaugh and Sam Holbrook in 1954, and Dick Heagy joined the business in 1955. Dick Kehoe was a partner for a short time. Burleigh Burgh bought Kehoe's interest in 1959, and when Deafenbaugh and Heagy decided to sell their interest in 1974, Burgh bought Heagy's one-third interest and Craig Smith bought Deafenbaugh's interest.

Although not open late at night like years ago, Breading's continues to be a favored downtown meeting place. The annual Breading's Christmas party "packs the house," and one can still stop by for an occasional game of dominoes.

This building was erected in the 1860s and was occupied by Yost's Cigar Store, where the famous "Bankable" cigars were made on the second floor. It later became Breading's Cigar Store. At the entrance is Terry Kloudaris, left, and Paul Latta, right (c. 1940s).

108

The new Breading Cigar Store was built right next to the old one. It was a "guy" place. As you walked in the front door, there was a counter for cigarettes and cigars. In the back was a counter with about ten round stools. In back of the guys sitting at the food counter were six or eight tables with four or five chairs around each. Guys played dominoes together all the time.

I worked the counter and made sandwiches and milkshakes and coffee. I also sold cigarettes and cigars. If someone playing at the table wanted a pack of Lucky Strike cigarettes, I would get it and throw it over to them.

We also had one of the few phones in town. The guys would often call home and say they'd be home after a while. We had one bathroom and one pinball machine.

Whenever you walked into Breading's, it was loudly announced, "Here is 'Blank Blank.' Remember the day he did 'blank blank'?" Good or bad. You were famous and accepted as a good guy.

They had the neatest way to wash dishes. There were three sinks side by side. The first sink had soapy water with brushes sticking up to put the glasses on and push down and up. The second sink was for rinsing with warm water. The third sink was filled with water with a drying mixture added to it. The water would run into the third sink and would slowly run over the top of the second sink and then over to the first. It would keep the water clean and clear all the time. Glasses were set off on a towel to dry quickly.

Me being the perfect cook and counter boy, I would have some fun when guys came in half asleep and sat at the counter. We had a water faucet with a lever that sat on top of the counter. Before anyone ordered, I would put a glass up there and fill it with water. The fun was that I set the glass up there upside down and pulled the lever so the water looked like it was filling the glass.

As I took it to the customer, I would bump the glass on the edge of the counter so it looked like I was spilling it and it was going to pour all down the front of the guest waiting on it. They were so surprised that sometimes they fell off of their stool backward. Was I great or what? There were a lot of fights at Breading's, but nobody was shot or killed.

Sam Holbrook and son

My dad would go to the Breading Cigar Store every night from nine to ten o'clock to play dominoes. The mayor, police, and lawyers all ate there. Sam Holbrook, who later became the town sheriff, worked with me there as well.

Age Fifteen

During high school, I got a job at Bledsoe Buick on West Center Street across from the Double Dip ice cream shop right next to the McCowen Cadillac/Olds dealership. My job was washing and waxing cars. Closer to when I was sixteen, Bledsoe's moved to a new, much bigger place north on Highway 15 (Detroit Street). Pioneer Auto Sales is at that location now. It was a big job moving all those auto parts out of there.

Dale, age fifteen

I had an electric power buffer to polish cars, so I got a job detailing cars at N&J Auto Sales, on the corner of Lake and Market Streets across from the post office. N&J had been in business longer than any other used car dealership in Warsaw. My mother worked at the Monument Works next to the post office and did engraving on tombstones.

Age Sixteen to Seventeen

I was a good student at school, but I refused to do homework. I would tell the teacher that I'd do what she wanted me to do at school, but when school was over for the day, I went to work to make money! When I turned sixteen, I paid cash for a 1950 red Chevy convertible. Girls started looking better to me, and I had a few dates with a nice girl from Atwood.

I had a classmate who was dating a girl from Mentone. I went on a blind double date with them and met Deanna Grubbs from Mentone.

1955

1950 red Chevy Convertible

My mother said I could only go to see Deanna on the weekends because of school. Soooo … during the school week, I would tell Mom I was driving uptown to see some of the guys, but instead, I would drive the fourteen miles down to see Deanna.

That worked great for a while, but then Mom started questioning me. Each morning during the week, after I had driven down to see Deanna, I would get up for breakfast and Mom would say, "It's Wednesday [or whatever day it was], and you were down at Deanna's last night. You are grounded until the weekend!"

What? From then on, every time I made the weeknight trip, I got grounded the next morning. I asked Deanna if her mother was calling my mom. There was no lipstick, no hickeys on my neck, no perfume, no hairs on me anywhere.

I took a different route down to see Deanna. I borrowed another guy's car and made the trip. I unhooked my odometer and plugged it back in when I got home. Nothing worked! I did not find out how Mom knew until fifty years later. Story to be continued …

I ended up marrying Deanna at the age of seventeen on what was called the "six-month free trial plan." Legally, to get married, a girl had to be sixteen, and the boy had to be eighteen. Since I was only seventeen, we had to take our mothers with us to see the judge first. He said we could get married in June of 1956, but it would not be legal until my eighteenth birthday in December 1956. He added that if it didn't work out for me, all I had to do was contact him and the marriage would be annulled at no cost.

Wow, was Deanna nice to me for a while! We were married on June 8, 1956, and stayed married for seventeen years.

Dale, age sixteen

Seventeen and Getting Married

Dale, age seventeen

I had one thing I needed to do before the wedding. I had worked my way up to parts manager at Bledsoe's and had traded my 1950 Chevy for a 1952 black Super-Buick with side skirts. It was a straight-eight engine with one exhaust pipe out the *left* side of the car. I wanted *dual* pipes out the back. Mom and Dad had said no. Deanna had also said no.

I rented an apartment at 604 East Center Street on June 1. I moved in and had duals put on the week before the wedding. The 1953 Buicks had V8 motors with the pipes coming out the *right* side, which was really what I wanted. Since I was the parts manager, I had access to those, which made it possible for Fred Boggs to use the good V8 pipes on the right side.

The pipes came out the back in Pontiac chrome bumper holders. The two mufflers were called *steel packs*. They made a deeper sound than the glass packs. The glass packs wore out too fast and were too loud after a while. It had a very deep sound like a big V12 motor. I would not let anyone look under the hood to see what was there.

Anyhow, we got married a few days later. It was a toss-up which I liked best—Deanna or the duals. P.S. We drove around a *lot* the next few days!

Work and Marriage

∿

Back to Bledsoe's

Bledsoe Buick bought out the Pontiac dealership, and John Hall and I had to move all the parts and the parts bins to Bledsoe's. In doing so, John got his arm cut wide open when one of the parts bins fell on his arm. I drove him to the hospital. We both remember that day!

Sometime during this period, I worked for Rush Wilson and Jim Bear at a new store on East Winona Avenue, just over the railroad tracks on the north side. It was called NAPA. I waited on customers at the counter. Russ was the shop guy, and Jim was the salesman.

NAPA later moved north on IN 15/Detroit Street in Warsaw. Jim would come in every morning and speak in German to me. "*RFSORSLXZNDEBLOCKENPHILHOSEV!*" He never told me what it meant.

While working at Bledsoe's, I also worked part-time at a gas station. The owner would pay his workers what he thought they were worth each week. The week I broke his lawn mower, I got paid less.

One week, he bent over and could not get straightened back up. I called his chiropractor to come over. Meanwhile, I took him to the car lift and ran it up for him to rest his arms on. That week, I got paid more.

When I worked there on evenings when it snowed, he had me stay outside and constantly walk back and forth with the snow shovel until a car pulled in. I pumped gas, cleaned the windows, checked the oil, put air in the tires, and took the money to the owner. He would make the change or use the credit-card system of those days. I would take the receipt or change back to the car and continue to push the snow shovel on the drive.

On Sundays, the gas station was all mine. We had a deal with Mr. Bledsoe next door that if someone stopped to look at a used car, I had field binoculars and was to get their license number and note which car they were looking at. On Monday, I gave the information to Bledsoe.

Back then, you could get the listing of the license number along with the car owner's address. He would have a salesperson get in the car they had looked at and drive it out to their home. He would tell them that this was just the car they needed and make a deal with them. I would follow the salesman and bring him back if the deal went well. We sold a lot of cars that way!

I traded cars at Bledsoe's again and got one that I had been waiting on for a long time: a 1954 white Super-Buick convertible with red leather seats. *Wow*, if I only had that car now! It had the three portholes in the front fenders, and I put lights in each one of them to stay on when I had my dims on.

College

As an eighteen-year-old parts manager at Bledsoe's Buick, part of my job was to take people to work or home when they brought their car in for a repair and needed a ride. I got to know a lot of people that way.

One man I would take to work was a professor of Christian theology, Dr. McClain. He was also the president of Grace College and Seminary in Winona Lake. The Grace

College campus was just a single large building called McClain Hall. The chapel as well as the classrooms and the offices were all in the same building.

Dr. McClain talked me into coming to college there, which I did that year. I had really wanted to go to Angola College instead. When I visited there, they had ashtrays on each desk. How cool would that be?

I was having trouble in math class. The instructor said I needed help and asked when I had a study period so that he could explain what I didn't understand. We met a bunch of times. The problem was, that was when I usually got in the car and drove out of town and smoked some cigarettes.

One day, I just didn't show up. I was sneaking out of class the next day when he called my name. When we met face to face, he said, "I believe there is an apology to be made here."

I didn't know what to say, so I didn't say anything. Then he said that he was sorry he didn't make it the day before. He suggested we take a break, and if I needed more help later, I could let him know. Now that was a Christian way to let me off the hook!

TR3

Bledsoe was wanting to add some sort of car that used less gas. Buick had taken on the Opel, a little four-cylinder car, and later a French Simca, which was about the same.

I was trying to get him to get some hot sports cars. I liked the Triumphs and really wanted a TR3. There was a dealer in Fort Wayne, so he told me to pick out the one I wanted and he would buy it and then sell it to me at dealer cost—if I would let him drive it each day to get the mail at the post office. *Deal!* I still wish I had kept the 1954 too! I would love driving that now.

The TR3 was two-passenger and sat so low that the doors had a big curve in them. You could sit in the seat and touch the ground or paint the line down the middle of the road. When you went to a Penguin Point or a root beer stand, they would set your tray on the ground.

Six months later, I went to work at R. R. Donnelley & Sons Printing Co. in Warsaw. This was a new printing plant that had just started up in Warsaw as a part of a large Chicago plant called Lake Side Press. They had about fifteen plants around the US. Each plant had its own specialty. Another plant in Indiana printed phone books. The Warsaw plant was more for catalogs like J. C. Penney, Land's End, Radio Shack, Western Auto, and Eddie Bauer. Five-foot rolls of paper for printing came in by train car.

Just about all the catalogs went out through the US Postal Service. This was before zip codes, and we had our own post office right in the plant. At that time, most mail went out by railroad cars going east or west.

Deanna and I with the TR3 and Oldsmobile we had in Delaware USAF

Deanna and I had moved into a new home in the Melody Acres addition about two miles from the plant. However, just before we moved, I was working the eleven p.m. to seven a.m. shift and would speed into town about seventy miles per hour in a forty-mile-per hour-speed-limit zone. One of those times, a policeman spotted me and came after me. I made a few quick turns and lost him.

I went home, and Deanna got in the car to go to work at the WRSW radio station. I sat home hoping the police would not see her going to work. Whew! No problem that time! It was the only little red sports car in town.

I was color blind, so I could not be involved with the five-color printing press at Donnelley's. Instead, I went to work as a checker. I would sit all day printing the name of towns on mailbag tags to be used as the catalogs were produced. There were thousands and thousands of tags, mostly for Western Auto stores all over the country. Again, this was before zip codes.

One very cold morning after working the night shift, I went to the parking lot, and very few cars would start. It was below zero. Everybody looked at me as I got into the TR3. I pulled the choke out, turned the key, and hit the starter—nothing! The guys laughed at me until I got out of the car, opened the small trunk, and pulled out a hand crank.

I walked around in front of the TR3. I pushed the crank in the small hole in the grill of the car and hand-cranked it clockwise, and the motor started. I surprised everybody!

TR3

Deanna and I had another couple we ran around with. They had a black two-passenger MGA sports car. These cars were being made in England. We would all four drive around with long cigarette holders, smoking like we were celebrities from some other country.

Military Service

The Vietnam War came along, and I enlisted in the United States Air Force in November of 1961. My basic training was for eight weeks in San Antonio, Texas. I came home for a week, and then I took the train to Philadelphia and the bus to the Dover, Delaware, Air Force Base where I was to be stationed. Deanna moved back with her mom and dad on a thousand-acre farm, and we rented the new house out.

Deanna stayed with her mom and dad until I got settled in Dover and rented a house trailer a mile or two out of town next to another trailer with a small Avon factory near it. We couldn't fit all of our clothes in our little TR3, so we got a 1953 four-door Olds and packed it full. Off we went to Dover. We left the TR3 with my dad, who sometimes drove it to work at Zimmer Manufacturing Company in Warsaw.

House trailer in Dover, Delaware

Deanna made friends with our neighbor, Lt. Frank Winfield, and his wife, Dorothy. They had two kids while we lived next to them. Then we moved to a nice trailer court and had new friends, Tom and Rhoda Doran. We played a lot of cards and collected old coins with them. We had a lot of fun together.

One time we went out for breakfast with them. A sign advertised one of anything *free*, so I ordered one of *everything* on the menu and ate it: one egg, one French fry, one slice of bacon, one slice of toast. The sign said one of *anything* free!

GRADUATE IN HONOR UNIT. — Six airmen from the Warsaw area display their squadron guidon with an honor pennant earned in basic military training at Lackland AFB, San Antonio, Tex. From left they are Max Clingaman, Bruce Mitterling, Frederick Zimmerman, Charles Hartman, Dale Long and Roger Bucher. Clingaman, son of Mr. and Mrs. Leon Clingaman, Sidney, has been assigned to communications school at Sheppard AFB, Wichita Falls, Tex.; Mitterling, son of Mr. and Mrs. Forrest Mitterling, Warsaw, is enrolled in a radar and radio maintenance course at Keesler AFB, Miss. Zimmerman, whose wife now resides in Crawfordsville, and Bucher, son of Mr. and Mrs. Gerald Bucher, Route 1, Akron, are in technical schools at Amarillo AFB, Tex., learning to be an administrative specialist and an aircraft and missile mechanic, respectively. Airman Hartman, son of Mr. and Mrs. Fred C. Hartman, Route 2, Warsaw, will transfer to an Ohio base. Dale Long, son of Mr. and Mrs. Merlin Long, Winona Beach, is also awaiting transfer. Dale will be trained in some phase of administrative work. — (Air Force Photo.)

Basic training in Texas. All these men were from Warsaw.

When I received my orders to go to Dover, my first thought was the white cliffs of Dover, England. No—Dover, Delaware! I was to go to base headquarters and report to Major Brunski. A major was just a little less than God to a guy with one stripe on his arm.

I went with two other guys like me to base headquarters. We walked down the hall until we saw an open door with a secretary sitting behind a desk. I tapped on the doorpost and asked where we could find Major Brunski. She looked up and said, "You have found her, airmen. Aren't you supposed to be doing something, airmen?"

"Yes ma'am!" I replied as I stood at attention and said, "Airman Third Class Long reporting as ordered."

Civil Air Patrol

Major Brunski picked me to work for her for three years. She made me Base Forms and Regulations Manager and gave me some goals to reach for, and then she assigned me the duty of maintaining the base regulations in the manual library and keeping it up to date.

The library was about the size of a three-car garage. I had a drafting table and a varia-typer to make the forms. It had all kinds of sizes and shapes of type, and it could make blocks of all sizes. I reduced the use of forms on the base by 75 percent and had pilots and other people thanking me for eliminating the form they had to fill out each day.

A month or so after I returned home, I received the USAF commendation medal for performing above and beyond the call of duty as Base Forms and Regulations Manager.

Base headquarters

Another one of my daily jobs was to play "The Star-Spangled Banner" in the morning on the loudspeaker as the air police raised the American flag. We repeated the process in the evening as the flag came down and was properly folded by the air police. It was sometimes a challenge when the flag was to be flown at half-mast to determine where that mark was, so I made a suggestion to put a round of duct tape on the exact spot. I made fifty dollars for that suggestion!

When foreign dignitaries arrived at the base, I was to play a "song of appropriate taste" as they passed the base headquarters. I only had five 78 rpm records, so my choices were very limited. One time I played "Waltzing Matilda." Surprisingly, no one complained about my choice.

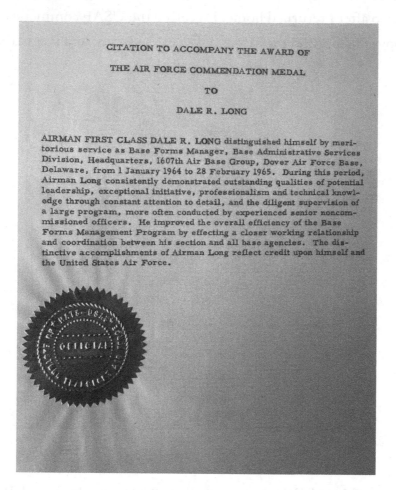

Major Brunski thought I was a great airman, so she submitted my name for the Airman of the Month award on the base. I had to go before a board of higher-ranking sergeants and officers who would ask each airman about twenty questions before making the decision.

I didn't make it, so she put me in again. Again, I didn't make it. She couldn't understand why I hadn't made it, so the next month she sat in on the board to see what was up. I didn't make it that time either!

She called me into her office the next day. She said I answered all the questions right except the last one. The question was, "Why do you think you should be Airman of the Month?" She said the only answer to that question is, "I am the best darn airman on the base."

I made it the next month.

Meeting the Vice President

Early in 1963, Deanna's mom and dad, Elsie and Herschel Grubbs, came to visit us for a few days. The day after they arrived, Vice President Lyndon Johnson landed at the base for a meeting somewhere in Delaware. We all went to watch as he came out of the plane.

As he was walking along the crowd of people, shaking hands with some of them, Elsie pushed her way through four rows of people, grabbed Johnson by the sleeve, and told him that they had driven all night just to see him! That was a bit of an exaggeration, because the Grubbs never voted and really didn't care *who* the vice president was. The Secret Service was quick to keep Johnson moving.

Then, to top it off, there was a parade to honor the vice president, with wooden barriers set up along the parade route. We all stayed behind the barricades as his car drove by—except Elsie, who decided to

USAF commendation medal

crawl under them and go out to see him again. Again, the Secret Service agents did their job well and stopped her.

I took a picture of the vice president pointing his finger at her as she started her move forward. Unfortunately, I didn't get to keep the picture for my file.

On November 22, 1963, President John F. Kennedy was shot in Dallas, Texas, by Lee Harvey Oswald. When this happened, the defense condition in the US dropped from a seven to a two. We had no idea what had happened. We were told to go out on the flight line, where we would be given M-1 rifles, and we were to get on a C-124 aircraft to go … somewhere. We had been told that if the US was ever attacked, we would probably see missiles coming over the base heading to Washington, DC.

It took the rest of the day to find out what had happened in Dallas. I finally got to leave the base and go home, about five miles from the base. The defense number had changed to four. When I got home to tell my wife what had happened, she said she had seen it live on TV that day.

That was Friday—her birthday. Two days later, we were watching all the replays of this tragic weekend when we saw Lee Harvey Oswald shot and killed on live TV as well.

Many years later, in my second marriage, we went to Dallas many times, and I went to the book depository area where JFK was shot and learned much more about what really happened in Dallas that day. It was like 9/11 in that you remembered exactly where you were and what you were doing when you heard the news.

Back Home

After putting in my four years at Dover and not being sent off to someplace where I might have been killed, I told God, "If you get me through this, I will stop smoking and drinking the day I sign out of the USAF." I kept my promise to Him, and I stopped both habits.

When we loaded the Oldsmobile to move back home, it was totally packed—so much that I could not get the trunk closed. I moved stuff around and slammed the lid hard. When we got home and lifted the trunk lid, there was more room. The trunk floor had rusted through and fallen down on the gas tank, and our clothes and everything else in the trunk were falling out.

We traded the TR3 on a GT6 and on to a TR6, which was really a great sports car. Then we made the big move. We got a silver Porsche 914 2.0 mid-engine that was really fun to drive. Now we had a Porsche 2.0 and a blue VW bug.

Me now   Me then

Down on the Farm

I helped out a lot on my in-laws' farm. We showed horses—gold Palomino quarter horses and others. I learned to do all the chores. Herschel Grubbs, my father-in-law, had a lot of hogs. He had three tractors, and I was allowed to do almost anything in the field except plow. That was Herschel's responsibility.

I had stayed at the farmhouse some nights before we were married. Herschel had a large gas tank with gas for tractors. He would have trouble with people stealing gas. One night, I was sleeping and heard a car or something pull into the drive.

Swish! Herschel was out the door, and I heard three or four shots. As he walked by my room, he said, "I'll read over them in the morning."

Just north of the farmhouse was a chicken processing plant with all kinds of people working there. On their lunch hour, they would often drive by the house and throw out their beer cans. Herschel would yell at them. They would just ignore him and go on.

One day, they drove by again and threw out their cans and went on down the road a mile or so. Herschel took out his shotgun and stood behind a tree when this nice white car came by and threw out some more cans. He stepped out in the road behind them and unloaded both barrels in the back of their car. That stopped the problem.

When the white car went by the next time, you could see that the back of the car was full of holes. Herschel had moved to Indiana from the West and still took action to solve a problem Western style!

Herschel had a very nice dog, and sometimes the chicken crates would fall off the truck headed to the processing plant and the dog would enjoy chasing them. This story will continue a little later.

Back at R. R. Donnelley's

After the USAF, Deanna and I lived in Melody Acres in Warsaw. I had gotten several promotions at R. R. Donnelley's. I was now a large bookbinder machine operator. It was a large, highly mechanical machine with a five-knife trimmer that put "books" (the individual pages of the catalogs) together and put in the staples. It could print individual store names on the finished catalogs as they went by, as well as stick an address label on each one. It required a fourteen-person crew and was about as long as it is from first base to third.

So this was my daily routine: I got up and drank a cup of coffee and then drove to R. R. Donnelley's in the Super-Beetle Volkswagen. Deanna would get up later and pack the laundry in the Porsche to take it down to the farm, which was about ten miles from our house, for her mother to do the wash.

I would get my lunch out of the vending machines at work, and then after work, I would drive the Volkswagen down to the farm to be a farmer. Elsie Grubbs would fix me supper. We did not need to keep food at our house. On days off and Saturdays and Sundays, we were always down at the farm anyway.

Each working day, I drove the VW about twenty miles. One day, after I'd had the oil changed in the VW, I backed out of the garage and spotted a small leak of oil. *Oh, I better check that out soon*, I thought as I drove off to work. I went to R. R. D and then down to the farm and forgot about the leak.

The next morning, the same thing happened. Two or three days went by before I remembered to check it. I dipped my finger into the "leak" and sniffed it. *Ooooh!* I knew the difference between engine oil and transmission oil and brake fluid, and it was none of those. That was from a chicken! (You can give me a call if you want the details.)

The chicken must have fallen off the truck on its way to the processing plant. The dog probably chased it around, and it got under the VW for protection. It got up in front of the VW motor and rode with me for several days.

I got a broom handle and went out on a dirt road and poked the chicken out. He headed down the road in bad shape, looking for another VW. True story!

The Grubbs wanted me to quit R. R. D. and farm. I liked to farm, but I was a people person. Sitting on a tractor all day looking for arrowheads as I went from row to row wasn't what I wanted to do with the rest of my life. Our marriage was shaky, and I actually left Deanna one time, but I came back when Herschel had a heart attack and they needed me.

I did the farming one whole year. The day after all the crops were planted, I packed all I needed in the VW and took a week's vacation. When I came back, I filed for divorce after seventeen years of marriage. We split everything evenly. She got the Porsche, and I got the VW.

Dale sitting on a tractor

A Mystery Solved

Dad died at age sixty-six after I came back from the USAF—just one year after he retired. (My brother also died at age sixty-six, so I was very glad when I had my sixty-seventh birthday!) Mom lived twenty-five more years and passed away in 2000 on the Fourth of July.

A short time before her passing, I asked her how she knew when I went down to Deanna's during the week. Remember, I promised I would tell you! Are you ready for this? Here is what she said: "On Saturday, you went down and picked her up to go to the movies. You stopped back by the house and went into the bedroom, and you put on a nice short-sleeve shirt. We three sat and talked for a while. Back then, it was cool for guys to roll up their sleeves a bit. Deanna sat beside you and rolled up your sleeves. Every time you would go down to see her, she rolled up your sleeves, and the next morning, there lay your shirt with your sleeves rolled up."

It took her fifty years to tell me that. When I looked back at pictures of Deanna and me, there were my sleeves rolled up! Check out my rolled-up sleeves in this picture.

Afterword

There you have it! I feel blessed to have grown up in Warsaw during the time in history that I did. May you treasure every moment and build wonderful memories to look back on the rest of your life as you move forward!

Before I end the reflection on this part of my life, I must go back to the question in the introduction: will there be a sequel to this book? That's yet to be determined, but this book isn't quite complete without a glimpse of what my future would hold.

After Karen and I were married in 1976, we were so thankful to have each other that we knew it was time to find a church where we could start our new life together with fellow believers. We had both grown up in church, but our first spouses were not Christ-centered, and we had slowly drifted away.

God led us to a church that was just right for where we found ourselves in life. We also joined a Sunday school class for young married couples—we were the oldest ones in the class, but we were the most newly married.

Like all married couples and families, we've certainly had our challenges in life—some rather small, and some so big that we didn't think we could make it through them. With God at the center of our marriage, our faith has remained steady, and we have grown even closer together. For that, we are most grateful!

Now, to begin the sequel …

Printed in the United States
by Baker & Taylor Publisher Services

Printed in the United States
by Baker & Taylor Publisher Services